Sports Stars

WALTER PAYTON

Record-Breaking Runner

By R. Conrad Stein

CHILDRENS PRESS®
CHICAGO

Cover photograph: Brian Fritz
Inside photographs courtesy of the following:
Brian Fritz, page 6
R.L. Montgomery, pages 8 and 23
Carl Sissac, pages 11, 15, 21, 30, 33, 36, 38, 41, 43, and 45
Bryan Yablonsky, pages 17, 19, and 35
Bill Smith Photography, page 26

Library of Congress Cataloging in Publication Data

Stein, R. Conrad.
  Walter Payton: record-breaking runner.

  (Sport stars)
  Summary: Traces the life of the professional football player
who broke the NFL's career rushing record in 1984
  1. Payton, Walter, 1954-   —Juvenile literature.
2. Football players—United States—Biography—
Juvenile literature. [1. Payton, Walter, 1954-   . 2. Football
players. 3. Afro-Americans—Biography.]
I. Title. II. Series.
GV939.P39S73   1987   796.332′092′4 [B] [92]   87-13241
ISBN 0-516-04363-3

      13 14 15 16 17 18 19 R 93 92

Sports Stars

WALTER PAYTON

Record-Breaking Runner

Waiting. Walter Payton *hates* to wait. He is a bundle of nervous energy. He cannot just sit still. He even plays chess standing up.

Once Walter had to wait in the Chicago Bears office. He noticed the telephone operator. She was behind in her calls. So the halfback sat next to her. He helped her.

Ring.

"Hello. This is the office of the Chicago Bears."

A pause.

"You want to speak with Coach Mike Ditka? Well, so do I. He's the guy I'm sitting around waiting for."

Fans love to watch Walter when he is running.

But all of us must wait for some things—even Walter. Walter was in his ninth year as a pro. The all-time rushing record loomed ahead of him. The rushing record was held by Hall of Fame running back Jim Brown. Breaking it would be a great feat. Walter was nearing his record-breaking run. The sports world was waiting with him.

The day finally came in October 1984. The Bears were playing the New Orleans Saints. Early in the second half, quarterback Jim McMahon called the play. He said, "Toss-28-Weak-the-2-back." That meant Walter was to run wide to the left behind a wall of blockers.

McMahon handed the ball off to No. 34. The halfback glided left. Then he spotted a tiny opening. He put his dead down. He drove forward—into history.

The play gained only a few yards. But when the bodies unpiled, the crowd burst into cheers. Cameras clicked madly. Photographers ran onto the field. Walter did it! Those couple of yards made Walter the most productive runner who ever played in the NFL.

But wait a minute. How seriously did Walter take all this? All the hoopla about breaking the record? After the game the locker-room telephone rang. It was President Ronald Reagan. He wanted to congratulate Walter. Walter smiled and mumbled something about income tax. Then he took the phone. He said, "The check is in the mail."

Walter holds the ball aloft after breaking Jim Brown's record, as the fans cheer.

Humor is a part of Walter's life. His former teammate, Matt Suhey, says, "I really don't think people realize what a great person Walter is. He's got a tremendous ego on the field, but he's also got a great sense of humor, an ability to say something light at the right time. When I dropped a pass against the Colts, on the way back to the huddle he said to me, 'You can always get a paper route or join the Army.' That loosened me up, and two plays later I scored a touchdown."

Walter's practical jokes are something. During the 1986 season the Bears hired quarterback Doug Flutie. Flutie stands only 5 feet 9 inches tall. He is short to be a quarterback. On his first day of practice, someone sneaked a tiny football onto the field. Doug Flutie's name was on it. Everyone agreed the jokester was Walter Payton.

Sometimes Walter's personality overshadows his athletic ability. He amused and amazed his former teammates. Once he stood on his hands. Then he balanced himself. He walked half the length of the football field.

He can dunk a basketball. He can do it wearing a full football uniform. Walter once crept up behind an assistant coach. He placed his hands on the man's shoulders. He leapfrogged over his head! The assistant was 6 feet 5 inches tall.

Walter is not a huge man. He is 5 feet 11 inches. He weighs about 202 pounds. But his body is covered with rock hard muscle. Early in his career a Bear coach said of Walter, "I just saw him in the locker room and I thought God must have taken a chisel and said, 'I'm gonna make me a halfback.'"

Walter is retired now, but when he played he went through a series of moves when he was running the ball. The moves worried his opponents. First he darted, like a spring uncoiled. If he broke through the line, he made a graceful stutter step. He claimed this deerlike leap helped him to look downfield. There he could see friendly blockers and enemy tacklers. When an opponent came near, he would dance right or left to avoid a tackle. O.J. Simpson once called Walter a "Ping-Pong runner."

But when he was surrounded, Walter would simply plow forward like a runaway truck. Walter says, "See the thing about defensive players is that they want to hit you as hard as

They are all over him, but Walter seems fine.

they can. They're obsessed with that. My coach at Jackson State, Bob Hill, always said, 'If you're going to die anyway, die hard, never die easy.' So, that's what I try to do."

Running the ball was only one part of Payton's game. He was also a punishing blocker. He was a sure-handed receiver. And he threw passes. Amazingly, Payton could throw well with both arms—left and right. Because of injuries to other players, he once was pressed into service as a quarterback. He did a good job. His coach, Mike Ditka says, "Without a doubt, Walter is the most complete football player I've ever seen."

Not only did Walter run, he also blocked, received, and threw passes!

Finally, Walter was the unquestioned leader of the Bear offensive squad. Late in the 1986 season the Bear offensive was struggling. The team won its games mainly on the strength of the savage defense. One Sunday afternoon a Soldier Field fan held up a sign. It said: "OFFENSE. WE'RE GOING TO THE SUPER BOWL. ARE YOU COMING WITH US?"

In the third quarter Walter pointed to the sign. He made his offensive teammates look at it. The squad then put together a touchdown drive. The touchdown won the game.

Of course, Walter did not become football's most amazing player overnight. It took endless days of practice. It took long nights of study. And, most painful of all, it took waiting.

One thing Walter hates to do is wait.

Walter grew up in the small town of Columbia, Mississippi. As a boy he was a good athlete. But no one expected him to become a superstar. In fact, the most exceptional athlete in Columbia was a fleet running back named Eddie Payton—Walter's older brother.

The first time Walter stood on his high school football field, it wasn't to play football. He played drums for the school band. Eddie was the star halfback on the team. "My mom didn't want us both playing," Walter explained. "So I played in the band. After Eddie graduated I decided I'd try out for the team."

He made the team. And in his first game he ran 60 yards for a touchdown.

All the Paytons are proud of Walter, including, left to right, his sister, his son Jarrett, his mother, and his wife.

After graduating from high school, Walter went to nearby Jackson State University. He had 64 college scholarship offers. But he chose to stay near home. At Jackson State he joined his brother Eddie in the backfield. Eddie later played in the NFL. But he never achieved his younger brother's honors.

Jackson State football fans still buzz about the amazing Walter Payton. In college he earned the nickname "Sweetness" for his "sweet" moves. After four college seasons, he averaged more than 6 yards per carry. He also punted and kicked both field goals and extra points. In all, he scored 464 points. That was the most ever for a college player.

Walter's Number 34 is now famous.

His last college season was 1974. He should have won the Heisman Trophy as the best college player that year. But newspaper reporters choose the Heisman winners. And few newsmen visit tiny Jackson State.

Pro scouts come to the small colleges, however. They shook their heads in wonder when they saw Walter run with a football. They liked the way Walter played very much. So Walter was the fourth player chosen in the 1975 college draft. Next stop—Chicago. The Chicago Bears at that time were not a winning team.

When Walter first reported to the Bears, he was quiet. He was not the outgoing, confident jokester he is today. He was a country boy amazed at big-city life. Around TV cameras he was painfully shy. Reporters grew impatient with him. He took so long to answer questions.

Also, Chicago fans worshipped the memory of another runner. That runner had played a few years before Walter arrived. He was Gale Sayers, a darting, twisting ball carrier. Sayers had the speed and grace of a greyhound. There was something electric about Sayers. When he took the ball, a strange silence came over the stadium. The fans knew that Sayers could score from any point on the field.

So, the young Walter Payton had to adjust. He had a new city, a new coach, and new teammates. He also had to compete with the Gale Sayers legend.

Walter's rookie year was a disappointment. He gained only 679 yards. He failed to make any NFL all rookie team.

It was difficult for Walter to follow after someone as good as Gale Sayers (right).

Walter's second year was great. He rushed for 1,390 yards. All running backs want to rush for at least 1,000 yards. Walter did, for every other year except 1982, the year a strike shortened the season to only 9 games, and 1987, his last season. Walter was happy with his first 1,000-yard season. He gave every blocker on his offensive line a gold watch. The inscription on the watches read:

THANKS FOR THE 1000
WALTER

"Football is a team game," Walter told reporters. "If I were Muhammad Ali in the ring all alone, I could take all the credit. But I'm running out of a backfield. I'm only as good as my offensive line lets me be."

In 1977, his third season, Walter exploded into stardom. He carried the ball a record 339 times.

He gained 1,852 yards. His greatest fame came on a foggy November Sunday. It was against the Minnesota Vikings. On the very first play he took a hand off. He ran 29 yards. No one guessed anything. But this was the start of the Great Walter Payton Show.

The first half of the game was almost all Walter. Walter went right. Walter went up the middle. Play after play the Viking defense knew No. 34 would get the ball. But they could not stop his slashing runs. By the end of the half, he had gained 144 yards.

Act Two of the Great Walter Payton Show began. He had a dazzling 19-yard run. Soon, just five minutes were left to play. Walter swept left. He straight-armed a defender. He darted down the sidelines for a 58-yard gain. The Great Walter Payton Show had ended. It was a tough Bear victory. And it was a new record. Walter had gained 275 yards. This was more than any other player had ever run with the ball in one game. The record stands to this day.

In the locker room, Walter thanked his teammates. They had helped him set the record. He did allow a little self-pride, however.

"Say, Walter," he was asked. "How would you defense Walter Payton?"

"Well," he laughed. "The night before the game I'd kidnap Walter Payton."

Walter's performance against Minnesota silenced his critics in Chicago. Since his rookie year, the fans had complained. "Yeah, that Payton looks pretty good, but he's no Gale Sayers." Finally those comparisons stopped. Walter won the fans' respect. In Chicago he no longer had to play in the shadow of the great Gale Sayers.

The Cowboys are always a hard team to beat, especially on their home field.

Walter led the Bears to the playoffs in 1977. Their opponent was the Dallas Cowboys. The Cowboys were a super team. It was no contest. The Cowboys simply bulled over the young Bears. But afterward, Dallas coach Tom Landry said, "You can't appreciate Walter Payton unless you are on the sidelines watching him. He's so strong. We were hitting him with two or three men. He's one of the great ones."

For the remainder of the 1970s and into the 1980s, the Bears were an uneven team. They depended too much on Walter. Too often their game plan was to give the ball to No. 34. They hoped he could carry the entire team. Walter became a marked man. Every man on the defensive team watched him alone. Not even the greatest running back in history can score points then.

Walter grew as an individual during his team's losing years. He returned to college. He earned a master's degree in communications. A dedicated family man, he watched his two children growing up. He once said, "My wedding day was the most truly satisfying day of my life."

In 1980 he signed a new contract making him the highest-paid player in the NFL. He invested his money wisely. Today he is a wealthy man who owns several restaurants.

He also lost his shyness. Walter became an engaging public speaker. People enjoyed listening to him. He was wealthy and famous, yet he could laugh at himself. Off the field, he did volunteer work with children. Through the years Walter was hailed as a genuine American hero.

Today Walter is a wealthy man.

But he had still not reached the Super Bowl. That is the ultimate goal for all pro football players. To achieve that goal he had to suffer. He had to do what he hates most, wait.

In 1982 Mike Ditka took over as coach of the Bears. Ditka threw temper tantrums on the sidelines. But Walter liked his confidence. He was the first Bear coach who told the team, "We're gonna win the Super Bowl." The Bears drafted a zany, but good, quarterback named Jim McMahon. They later added a wide receiver, Willie Gault. He was one of the fastest men in the world. The Bears defensive squad became the most feared unit in the league. It was led by linebacker Mike Singletary and linemen Dan Hampton and Richard Dent.

Walter likes the confidence of his coach, Mike Ditka.

Sometimes even the referee gets trounced.

The 1984 Bears won 10 games and lost only 6. They earned a spot in the playoffs. The tough Washington Redskins were their first opponent. Walter opened the game by faking a run. Then he threw a 19-yard touchdown pass. Next, speedster Willie Gault took a short pass. He raced 75 yards to the end zone. The Bears beat Washington, 23 to 19.

However, their next game was against the powerful San Francisco 49ers. The 49ers trounced the Bears, 23-0. The Bears players remembered that loss all year. And for Walter Payton, it meant the frustrating wait for a Super Bowl appearance had to continue. He watched the 49ers go on and win the Super Bowl.

In 1986, the fans saluted Walter after he gained over 15,000 yards rushing.

A glorious year for the Bears and their fans followed. The team crushed its opposition in 1985. The Bears finished the regular season with 15 wins against only 1 loss. In the playoffs no one could stop them. They pounded the Giants. Then they pounded the Rams. Neither team scored a point against the Bears marvelous defensive squad.

Next stop—New Orleans and the Super Bowl.

For Walter Payton, the long wait had finally ended. The players of Super Bowl XX were introduced. Walter drew the wildest applause. The game itself was a runaway. The Bears beat the New England Patriots, 46 to 10. Walter did not seem to be the star of the game. Some reporters claimed he was pouting at the end. He had failed to score a touchdown. Walter later explained he was not pouting at all. He was just disappointed. The game was too easy.

Walter's twelfth season as a pro came in 1986. It is almost unheard of for a running back to be able to play so long. Walter has stayed in perfect physical condition all the time. He also has a high tolerance for pain. Midway through the 1986 season, he dislocated his big toe. Most players would have missed a few games. But Walter only missed a few plays.

The Bears finished with 14 victories and 2 losses in 1986. They had their sights set on another Super Bowl. But then they lost their

Walter poses with some of William Perry's supporters, the Refrigerettes.

first playoff game, to Washington. It was a bitter blow for the team. Many football experts had called the Bears one of history's best teams of all time.

Early in 1987 Walter made his ninth appearance in the annual Pro Bowl. During the game he broke O.J. Simpson's Pro Bowl rushing record. Walter now holds almost every pro football running record.

The Pro Bowl is played in Hawaii. In between practice sessions players relax at the beach. Nevertheless, most of the fans who came to meet the players clustered around Walter.

Walter sports his nickname "Sweetness" on his towel.

In 1987, Walter played his last year of pro football. And how did he finish? With more records than any pro football player ever.

Most yards gained—16,565. Most yards gained in a game—275. Most touchdowns—108. Most rushing attempts—3,601. Most seasons 1,000-yards-or-more—10. Most consecutive seasons 1,000-yards-or-more—6. Most games 100-or-more-yards—77. Most consecutive 100-yard games—9. Most combined net yards gained—21,601. Most consecutive games—184. Most consecutive starts—178. The list goes on and on.

And what will Walter Payton do next? "It has always been a dream of mine to own a franchise," he says. Own his own pro football team? Yes, that's what he wants next. Besides all the restaurants and other businesses he is involved in. "I've played the game of football all my life and there are some things I'd like to see changed," he says.

Having broken the records of other players, Walter set new records that future football players will have a hard time breaking.

CHRONOLOGY

1954 —Walter Payton is born in Columbia, Mississippi on July 25.

1961 —At the age of seven Walter starts playing the drums. Drumming will remain his favorite hobby.

1965 —Gale Sayers joins the Chicago Bears and becomes a local hero. Ten years later Chicago fans would expect Walter to become as good a running back as Sayers.

1967 —Walter starts Columbia High School, but he does not join the football team. Instead he is a drummer in the school band.

1969 —During his junior year Walter decides to play high school football. In his first game he runs 60 yards for a touchdown.

1971 —Walter enters Jackson State College.

1973 —While Walter is a junior in college, O.J. Simpson rushes for a record 2,000 yards with the Buffalo Bills. Payton would challenge that record four years later.

1974 —At the conclusion of his college career Walter has totaled 464 points scored to set a college record.

1975
Feb. —Walter is graduated from Jackson State College.

Sept.—Payton starts as halfback for the Chicago Bears.

1976
Nov. —Walter leads the NFL in running. It appears he will win the rushing title.

Dec. —On his most disappointing day as a football player Payton is unable to move the ball against the strong Denver Bronco defense and loses the rushing title to O.J. Simpson.

1977
Nov. —Walter runs for 275 yards in a game against Minnesota. This breaks the single-game rushing record established the year before by O.J. Simpson.

Dec. —In overtime the Bears beat the New York Giants 12-9 to enter the playoff. Payton finishes the year with 1,852 yards gained, 16 touchdowns, and 96 points. All these are league-leading totals.

1978 —At the Pro Bowl Walter accepts the Most Valuable Player award. He also scores the winning touchdown and is elected MVP of the Pro Bowl even though he claims his playing was "mediocre."

1983 —Walter becomes the fourth NFL rusher to gain 11,000 yards.

1984 —Walter exceeds Jim Brown's record by 997 yards, with a total of 13,309 yards gained rushing.

85   —Walter, quarterback Jim McMahon, and a savage defense lead the Bears to a 16-1 season. Walter scores 11 touchdowns and rushes for 1,551 yards.

86   —Early in the season, Walter surpasses 15,000 yards rushing and scores his 100th touchdown. Walter plays in his first Super Bowl. The Bears dominate New England, but Walter is used mostly as a decoy during the game.

87   —Walter plays in his ninth Pro Bowl, tying a record for All-Star appearances.

    —Walter Payton retires with more records and honors than any player in football history.

ABOUT THE AUTHOR

In his youth Mr. Stein was a mediocre basketball player, a poor baseball player, and an absolute disaster as a football player. Consequently, he spent many hours on the sidelines of athletic fields watching more gifted athletes perform. From an early age he became a fan.

Mr. Stein was especially pleased when Childrens Press asked him to write this book on Walter Payton. Mr. Stein was born and grew up in a Chicago neighborhood that was just a few blocks from Wrigley Field, where the Chicago Bears used to play ball. Mr. Stein is a lifelong Chicago Bear fan, and thinks that Walter Payton is the greatest running back in history.